Canning and Preserving for Beginners

The Ultimate Guide to Canning and Preserving Food

Table of Contents

Introduction 6

Chapter 1: Home Canning and Its Benefits 8

    The Benefits of Canning and Preserving Your Own Food. 8

    Reasons Why People Can 10

Chapter 2: What You Need To Know About Home Canning 13

    Techniques in Home Canning 13

        Technique #1 – Water Bath Technique 14

        Technique #2 – Pressure Canning Technique 16

    How to Choose the Right Processing Time 18

        Water Bath Canning 19

        Pressure Canning 20

    Other Factors That Involve Successful Canning 22

        Careful Selection and Preparation of Food 23

        Packing Style of Food 23

        Jar Preparation 24

        Adding Acids to Food 25

Chapter 3: Tips on How to Make High Quality Canned Foods 27

Quality of Food Used 27

Maintaining Flavor and Color of Canned Food 28

Containers 29

Storing the Finished Products 32

Dealing With Spoiled Canned Preserves 32

Chapter 4: How to Prepare Healthy Canned Foods 34

Canning without Using Sugar 34

Canning with Less Salt..35

Canning Baby Foods 35

Conclusion 36

Introduction

Canning and preserving are methods in improving the shelf life of food and preventing them from spoiling. In fact, many homes a hundred years ago rely on canning and preserving so that they can sustain their needs during periods of famine such as during the winter months or when there is a dry spell. However, with the presence of refrigeration, canning and preserving is no longer done by many people.

Home canning has come a long way from its early beginnings. Canning began when Frenchman Nicolas Appert discovered in 1795 that food sealed inside glass bottles and subjected under heat can last for a long time. Having said this, people during the 18th century towards early 19th century preserved their foods in ceramic crocks or glass bottles to keep meats, fruits and vegetables from spoiling. It was only in 1810 when Englishman Peter Durand developed ways on how to can food inside tin cans which led to the big canning industry.

Home canning was still a popular means of preserving food and many do home canning as a family chore. Most people preserve fruits and vegetables that they have harvested from their gardens so that they can have stash of food during the rainy days. However it was after World War II when home canning declined as a family chore. Unfortunately, people became too busy with their jobs that they no longer had the time to can their own foods. Moreover, buying tin canned foods at local grocery stores became a norm during that time.

Although the canning industry provides us with canned foods that can stay inside our pantries for a long time, learning how to do home canning is an essential skill everyone must know. This is especially true if you are planning to live in a sustainable household.

Chapter 1: Home Canning and Its Benefits

Home canning is a great activity that you can do to extend the shelf life of your food. Aside from increasing the shelf life, there are also many other reasons why home canning is a skill that everyone should learn. This chapter will discuss about the many benefits as well as reasons why people should do home canning.

The Benefits of Canning and Preserving Your Own Food

Home canning and preserving are one of the methods to protect your food from spoilage. Although modern refrigeration technology allows us to keep our foods fresh for a few weeks, canning and preserving can help increase the lifespan of food longer than refrigeration. Moreover, canned foods do not rely on electricity so they don't spoil even if you have an emergency power blackout for two days. If you haven't started canning then now is the time that you should. Below are the benefits of canning that will convince you to start today.

- **Convenience:** Canning allows you to build a pantry full of homemade foods that can fit in your busy lifestyle.
- **Steady supply of homegrown foods:** Although you can buy factory canned fruits and vegetables from your local grocery stores, you really don't have any idea of the kinds of ingredients that they put in the preserved foods. If you do home canning, you have a stock of fresh and homegrown foods that are not only delicious but also healthy.
- **Savings on food costs:** The purpose of home canning and preserving is to help you save on food costs. Since you take advantage of fresh food when they are in abundance, you end up saving a lot on your food costs.
- **Home canning is a fun activity to do:** Home canning is a chore that the entire family can enjoy. You can do home canning to teach other members of the family on how to be sustainable and not depend too much on store-bought foods.
- **Achieve a sense of fulfillment:** People who home can find sense of fulfillment knowing

that they are serving their families foods that you know are healthy.
- **You are in control:** Home canning and preserving requires you to use natural preservatives such as vinegar, sugar and salt. But since you are doing the canning yourself, you can control the amount of sugar, salt and vinegar that you use to preserve your food. Unlike store-bought canned foods, you do not have any idea how much sugar or salt they use to preserve food.

There are many benefits of canning your own food. You benefit from having more food choices, stable supply in your pantry and good overall health for the family. Having said this, it is important that you learn this very important skill so that your entire household can benefit from it.

Reasons Why People Can

There is a rising movement of home canning in America and one of the main reasons why people do home canning is that it is the easiest and most frugal ways to preserve high quality food and prevent them from spoiling. Canning your own food can also save you about half the cost compared to buying canned foods made from factories. Another reason why people do home canning is that products of home canning are healthier than store-bought canned foods. Below are the other reasons why people opt to do home canning instead of buy canned foods from the store:

- **Home canned foods are healthier:** Home canned foods are healthier versions of commercially canned products. They are low in sodium and are MSG free.

- **Altered to match your taste preference:** Another good reason why people do home canning is that they can alter the flavor of their canned and preserved foods to match the exact taste preference of the entire family. Thus, it is easier to convince everyone in the family to eat the canned foods that you have made.

- **It is frugal:** Home canning is very frugal and it can help you save a lot of money if you preserve your own food. Developing a frugal mindset is also very easy if you do home canning. In fact, some people who do home canning are encouraged to grow their own food by planting their own garden. Moreover, people who adopt other sustainable lifestyles are also into this particular home chore.

- **Preserved foods make great gifts:** If you are running out of ideas on what gifts to give your friends or loved ones during Christmas or any special occasion, then you can give your canned products instead. Giving a basket of canned goods is a simple yet elegant way of saying that you care for other people.

There are many reasons why people do home canning. While some people do home canning for health reasons, others just want to save money. Whatever your reasons are, home canning is one great skill that will help you achieve independence and sustainability.

Chapter 2: What You Need To Know About Home Canning

Although home canning dwindled during the mid-1900s, it is certainly on the rise now that many people are looking for ways on how to eat healthy as well as live sustainably. Statistics show that one in four households in the United States do home canning for their own personal use. In fact, the rising number of people who have seen the benefits of eating locally is also the reason why home canning is being revived in many households in the country. This chapter will deal with the technical side of home canning.

Techniques in Home Canning

You don't need to invest in very expensive equipment if you are planning to can your own food right at the comforts of your own home. In fact, you can use ordinary kitchen tools and implements to start canning your food. This section will discuss about the different techniques in home canning and preserving:

Technique #1 – Water Bath Technique

This technique is great when you are dealing with foods with high acid content. Thus, if you are planning to can fruit juices, salsas, tomatoes, pickles, chutneys, sauces, fruit spreads, jams, jellies and relishes, then this. Below is a detailed guide on how you can properly do canning using the water bath technique. To can successfully using the water bath technique, you will need the following things:

- Prepared preserved recipe such as chutney, jams and jellies or fresh produce
- Boiling water bath canner
- Glass preserving jars with metal lids
- Kitchen utensils like funnel, ladle and wooden spoon
- Kitchen mittens

Water bath canners are pots that are made from either porcelain-covered steel or aluminum. They have perforated racks that are removable where you can safely place the bottles. If you do not have a boiling water canner, you can improvise by getting a large saucepot with a lid. Place a rack at the bottom of the saucepot where the bottles of preserved foods or produce will be placed.

1.) Fill the water bath canner halfway with clean water. This is a level required when you load pint jars. However, for other sizes of jars, it is important to take note that the amount of water in the canner should be adjusted such that it will be 1 to 2 inches over the top of the filled jars.
2.) Preheat the water. If you are preserving raw foods, preheat it to 140^0F while preheat it to 180^0F if you are dealing with hot-packed foods.
3.) Load the filled jars with fitted lids to the canner and use a jar handler to lower them to the rack filled with water. Make sure that the jars remain in an upright position at all times as tilting can cause food to spill which can cause entry of air and eventually spoiling. Make sure that the bottled are tightly closed and free of air bubbles before submerging inside the water bath canner.
4.) Add more boiling water if necessary to maintain the 1 inch of water above the jar tops.
5.) Turn heat to high and cover the water bath canner with the lid.
6.) Set a timer for the total minutes needed to process the food. Make sure that the canner is covered at all times. Maintaining a boil all

throughout the process is also very important. You can adjust the heat setting to maintain boiling.

7.) Add more boiling water if needed if the water level evaporates. Make sure to maintain the 1 to 2 inches of water above the bottles.

8.) Turn off the heat once the bottles have been boiled for the recommended time. Wait for 5 minutes before removing the jars from the water bath canner.

9.) Use a jar lifter to remove the jar and place them on a towel. Let the jar cool undisturbed for 12 to 24 hours.

Technique #2 – Pressure Canning Technique

Another technique that you need to know when it comes to canning food is the pressure canning technique. This technique is great in preserving vegetables, meats such as poultry, pork, beef and seafood. The reason why pressure canning is done on meats is to also sterilize and remove any pathogens like bacteria or virus that can cause the food to easily spoil. Pressure canning technique can heat food to 240^0F. Below is the correct procedure on how to can using pressure canning technique.

1.) Pour 2 to 3 inches of hot water inside the pressure canner.
2.) Place the filled jars on the rack and make sure that they secured in place. Keep the jar upright at all times.
3.) Fasten the lid of the pressure canner securely.
4.) Leave the weight off the vent port of the pressure canner.
5.) Turn on the heat and heat at the highest setting until the steam flows from the vent port. Let the steam flow freely from the vent port for 10 minutes and place the weight back and let the can pressurize for the next 3 to 5 minutes.
6.) Start timing once the dial gauge of the pressure canner reaches the recommended pressure reading.
7.) Regular the heat under the canner to maintain and maintain a steady pressure. Follow the manufacturer's direction on how the weighted gauge works in maintaining the desired pressure.
8.) Once the process is complete, turn the heat off and remove the canner from the heat. Let the canner depressurize. Don't force open the pressure canner if it hasn't depressurized

completely otherwise the drastic change in pressure may cause the seal failures in the jar.
9.) After the canner has depressurized completely, remove the weight from the port and wait for 10 to 20 minutes before you unfasten and completely remove the lid.
10.) Remove the jars using the jar filter and place them in the towel. Leave 1 inch space between the jars while cooling and let them sit undisturbed for 12 to 24 hours at cool temperature.

Pressure canning is more challenging than water bath canning. And if not done properly, you may end up having problems with your canned foods. Spoiling occurs even if you do pressure canning because the internal canner temperature is lower than necessary. Another reason is the air trapped inside the preserved food can lower the temperature. This is the reason why it is important that you know about the necessary processing time of different foods when canning.

How to Choose the Right Processing Time

Selecting the right processing time is very important. This is to ensure that canning will be successful and that your canned food will not spoil easily even if you store it at room temperature for a long time. It is important to take note that the correct canning process largely depends on the type of food that you want to preserve and the size of the preserving jar or bottle. This is the reason why people who do home canning need to know about the different processing time to avoid their preserved foods from spoiling. This section will serve as your guide in determining the correct processing time to become successful in canning different types of food.

Water Bath Canning

Preserving food using water bath canning technique can be very challenging. The thing is that you need to use different temperature settings for different foods that you want to preserve. Moreover, the altitude as well as the size of the jar also affects the duration of processing time. To easily understand the correct processing time for water bath canning, a table summary is provided below:

Table 1: Correct processing time for water bath canning corresponding to the type of food material used size of jar and altitude.

Style of pack	Size of jar	0-1,000 ft*	1,001-3,000 ft*	3,001-6,000 ft*	Above 6,000 ft*
Hot	Pint	20	25	30	35
	Quarts	25	30	35	40
Raw	Pint	25	30	35	40
	Quarts	30	35	40	45

Process time with corresponding to different altitudes (minutes)

* Unit of altitude is feet above sea level.

Pressure Canning

There are different ways to do pressure canning and while some conventionally use weight-gauge pressure canning, others use dial-gauge. Different types of pressure canners also have different rules when it comes to selecting the right processing time. This is the reason why it is important to know how to choose the right processing time for both dial-gauge and weight-gauge pressure canning. Below are table summaries on how to choose the right processing time for the two pressure canning methods:

Table 2: Correct processing time for dial-gauge pressure canning corresponding to the type of food material used size of jar and altitude.

Style of pack	Size of jar	Processing time (mins)	0-1,000 ft	1,001-3,000 ft	3,001-6,000 ft	Above 6,000 ft
Hot	Pint	10	6	7	8	9
Raw	Quarts					

Table 3: Correct processing time for weight-gauge pressure canning corresponding to the type of food material used, size of jar and altitude.

Style of pack	Size of jar	Processing time (mins)	Required canner pressure (PSI) at corresponding altitudes (in pounds, lbs.)	
			0-1,000 ft	Above 1,000 ft
Hot	Pint	10	5	10
Raw	Quarts			

Other Factors That Involve Successful Canning

Canning is the most economical way to preserve the quality of food that you prepare at home. However, there is more to canning than just processing foods under high heat. In fact, if you want to learn canning, it is important that you also know that proper home canning includes the following:

Careful Selection and Preparation of Food

Food contains Oxygen and enzymes that can feed microorganisms so that they multiply quickly on the surface as well as inside. However, you can become successful in canning if you select foods that are fresh and free from damage. As much as possible, avoid canning foods that are bruised, insect-damaged or show signs of fungal diseases because they are very difficult to sterilize through canning. By selecting fresh foods, you will also be able to make sure that you only lose minimal amounts of vitamins and nutrients once you process your food.

Packing Style of Food

There are two ways to pack food through canning and preserving and these include raw packing and hot packing. Below is a discussion regarding the difference of both terms:

- **Raw packing**: This involves filling the jars with fresh and unheated food. Raw packing is a common packing technique suitable for canning vegetables inside a pressure canner. The downside to raw packing is that it encourages Oxygen from inside the tissues of food to mix in the liquid. Once the air is trapped and surrounds the food, it will cause discoloration of food within 3 months during storage. However, this will not affect the taste of the food at all.

- **Hot packing**: Hot packing involves heating food through boiling or simmering before they are packed into jars. This practice helps in removing the air found inside the food tissues. While the food shrinks after heating, it prevents the food from floating inside the preserved jar so you can fill more food inside the jar thus saving space.

Jar Preparation

Jar preparation is very crucial in successful canning. Moreover, the types of jars and sealing lids will also affect your canning success. Below are the important things that you need to know when it comes to jar preparation:

- Clean the jar thoroughly using a detergent soap. To remove the residue, soak the jar for 30 minutes in a water solution mixed with 1 cup vinegar.

- Sterilize clean jars prior to canning by submerging them in boiling water for at least 10 minutes.
- Use self-sealing lid with a gasket compound to ensure that the bottle will have a vacuum environment after canning.
- Make sure that you invest in jars that have lids that are secure. It will also make you successful if you don't recycle the lids. Recycling lids reduces its capability to achieve a totally vacuum environment necessary for preserving food. Eventually air has a tendency to enter inside the bottle during and after the canning process if the lids are recycled.

Adding Acids to Food

Adding acids to food such as vinegar or lemon juice can also improve the shelf life of the food after canning compared to foods that are not added with preservatives and are directly canned. This is the reason why canned foods added with acids have longer shelf lives than those that are not added with acids.

It is crucial to take note that all of these factors help destroy enzymes, remove Oxygen and inhibit the growth of pathogens like yeast, molds and the dreaded *Clostridium botulinum* that may cause many health problems.

Chapter 3: Tips on How to Make High Quality Canned Foods

Canning is a great skill that you need to learn today but it takes a lot of patience and practice to get it right. In fact, many people who are hooked to canning started with a lot of failures thus you should not feel discouraged once you end up having a few of your bottles spoiled. While spoiled preserves are common among those who are starting, it can be avoided if you know the right tips and tricks. This chapter will teach you on what you need to do to make high quality canned foods minus a lot of spoiling in your preserved batches.

Quality of Food Used

The quality of food used is very important when canning. Start with good quality foods that are suitable for canning. It is important to take note that not all kinds of foods are great for canning. To be successful in canning, below are the things that you need to know about food quality.

- Examine the food and make sure that they are fresh and not affected with diseases like spots and molds. If you still want to can foods that have diseases, discard the diseased spots or lesions using a clean kitchen knife.
- Whether you plan to can foods from your garden or bought from a local farmer, make sure to can then within 6 to 12 hours upon harvest of purchase. If you plan to delay your canning for a few more hours, make sure that you store your produce in a cool and shady place.
- Freshly slaughtered red meats as well as poultry should be canned immediately. Avoid canning meat from diseased animals. For fish, remove the entrails first and can them within two days.

Maintaining Flavor and Color of Canned Food

When you can your food, the color usually changes because the food is subjected to high heat. Although the color and flavor might be affected, there are ways for you to maintain these two things in your canned food.

- Make sure to remove the bubbles or Oxygen from the food itself as well as the jar. You can do this by hot packing the food.
- Destroy the food enzymes that can cause discoloration on the food through heat.
- Get jars that have airtight seals.
- Limit the time of exposure of your prepared food to air. If you must, can them once you have finished preparing them.
- For apples, nectarines, peaches, apricots and pears, soak them in a solution of water and ascorbic acid. You can also use other vitamin C tables or commercially prepared mixes of citric acid to prevent discoloration on your produce during the preparation.

Containers

Food may be canned in glass bottles or even metal containers. Most people who home can opt for wide-mouth Mason jars with self-sealing lids because they create tight vacuum air space during the canning process. However, other types of jars are fine. Below are the tips on how to have high quality canned foods using the right bottling techniques.

- Sterilize the containers prior to filling them with food for canning. Soak them in water mixed with a cup of vinegar before boiling them for 10 minutes.
- Fill hot foods inside the jar and adjust the headspace. The headspace refers to the unfilled space above the food inside the jar. Different types of foods require different headspace. Below is a list of food with their corresponding headspace:
  - Jellies and jams require ¼-inch headspace
  - Fruits and tomatoes processed in boiling water require ½-inch headspace
  - Low acid foods such as vegetables require 1 to 1 ¼-inches headspace especially when processed inside a pressure canner.
- The key to controlling the headspace is to take note of the air expansion that occurs during the canning process. At higher temperatures, the air expands more thus it is important to leave a lot of headspace especially if you are using pressure canning.
- Before closing the lid, make sure to wipe the upper rim of the jar with a clean cloth to remove moisture. This removes moisture

around the rim that might cause some air outside to penetrate the container.
- Tighten the screw bands securely in place but avoid over tightening the lid as possible.
- Make sure that the jars do not tilt during the entire processing time.
- Once you remove the hot jars from your canner, never retighten the lids because it will cut through the gasket thus causing seal failures. Instead, let the jars cool at room temperature for 24 hours so that the jar naturally loses the air and creates a tight vacuum seal.
- Test the jar seals once they have cooled. There are many ways that you can test if the seals are secured in place. First, you can press the middle of the lid with your thumb and once it springs up, then the lid is not properly sealed. Another thing that you can do is to tap the lid with a bottom of a teaspoon and if creates a dull sound, then it is sealed. A properly sealed bottle creates a high-pitched sound.
- If the lid does not seal properly on the jar after canning, remove the lid and examine the jar sealing if it has tiny cracks. If there are cracks, change the jar and reprocess the food within 24 hours.

Storing the Finished Products

Once you have checked that the jars are vacuum sealed, remove the screw bands and wash the lid as well as the jar to remove any food residue. Dry them using a clean kitchen towel. It is important that you label the jars with their name and processing date and store them inside a cool, dry and ark place. If you store your canned foods in places that have temperature exceeding to 95⁰F, the food will easily lose quality within a few weeks. Never freeze unopened jars because the moisture inside the fridge will make the metal lids corrode. However, if you need to freeze them, make sure that you wrap them in newspapers or any moisture-absorbing material to prevent the metals from corroding and damaging your seal.

Dealing With Spoiled Canned Preserves

Although you were confident that all of your canned products are tightly sealed, there will be one jar that will go bad. What happens when your canned food gets spoiled is that bacteria and yeast gets inside the jar and produces gas. The buildup of gas swells the lid and eventually breaks up the jar seal. Carefully preserved foods do not contain bubbles and if your canned foods contain bubbles, it is indication that it is going bad. Below are the tips on how to deal with spoiled canned foods so that you prevent feeding yourself and your family with food laced with deadly bacterial toxins.

- Place the suspected sealed glass jars inside a sealed garbage bag and dispose immediately.
- If the suspected jars are unsealed or opened, it is important to detoxify it to remove the presence of the bacteria *Clostridium.*
- When sterilizing contaminated jars, it is important that you carefully treat the contaminated jars by placing the contents inside a trash bag and throwing it away immediately.
- Boil the contaminated jar in boiling water for 30 minutes.
- Make sure that you clean up the area because the bacterial spores of *Clostridium botulinum* can be fatal when ingested. Spray your table and stove top with a bleach solution.

Chapter 4: How to Prepare Healthy Canned Foods

Commercially canned foods contain more salt and sugar and this is the reason why home canning is preferred by many because they have control over the amount of sugar and salt that they put in their food. There are many conventional canning recipes that you can make but this book will discuss about healthy canned foods that you can prepare. This is especially true if you live with someone who is required to eat foods less in sugar and salt. This chapter will give you a detailed discussion on the different types of healthy canned food recipes that you can do at home.

Canning without Using Sugar

Conventional canning methods require the use of sugar to preserve food for a long time. But didn't you know that you can still can and preserve food without using sugar? In canning fruits without sugar, it is important to select fruits that are firm but fully ripe. Avoid choosing fruits that show signs of diseases. Prepare the fruits for hot packs and use unsweetened fruit juices or just regular water to add sweetness to the fruit. However, if you like your preserved fruits sweet, you can always use sugar substitute Splenda© before you process the food for canning.

Canning with Less Salt

Salt serves as a preservative for most foods including meats. If you don't want to use a lot of salt when canning your food because of diet restrictions, then you can still do so without fearing that your food will spoil. The thing is that salt used to can vegetables and meats are used primarily to enhance the flavor and not act as a preservative.

Canning Baby Foods

Baby foods can also be canned so that you can have a stash of prepared meals for your baby each day. You can prepare chunk-style or pureed fruits of your choice and make sure that you follow the appropriate processing time as indicated in Chapter 2. However, do not attempt to can pureed meats and vegetables because the processing time has not been determined for home use yet.

Conclusion

Canning is one of the most essential skills that you need to know so that you can prepare healthy foods for your family. It is a skill that will help many people save money on their grocery costs and, at the same, decrease their dependence on store-bought canned foods that are laden with sugar and salt. So if you are still deciding to take on canning as a new and sustaining hobby that your family can enjoy, then now is the time that you start. You will surely enjoy the many benefits that canning and preserving foods can give you through time.

Copyright © 2015. All rights reserved.

Except as permitted under the United States Copyright Act of 1976, reproduction or utilization of this work in any form or by any electronic, mechanical, or other means, now known or hereafter invented, including xerography, photocopying, and recording, and in any information storage and retrieval system, is forbidden without written permission.

The ideas, concepts, and opinions expressed in this book are intended to be used for educational and reference purposes only. Author and publisher claim no responsibility to any person or entity for any liability, loss, or damage caused or alleged to be caused directly or indirectly as a result of the use, application, or interpretation of the material in this book.

Made in the USA
Lexington, KY
15 December 2015